I'm Feeling... SCARED

Published 2012 by
A&C Black
An imprint of Bloomsbury Publishing Plc
50 Bedford Square, London, WC1B 3DP

www.acblack.com
www.bloomsbury.com

ISBN 978-1-4081-7183-7

Illustrations: Christiane Engel
Series consultant: Sally Featherstone

A CIP catalogue for this book is available from the British Library.

This book is produced using paper that is made from wood grown in managed, sustainable forests. It is natural, renewable and recyclable. The logging and manufacturing processes conform to the environmental regulations of the country of origin.

Printed in China by C&C Offset Printer Co.

10 9 8 7 6 5 4 3 2 1

I'm Feeling... SCARED

By Lisa Regan

Illustrated by Christiane Engel

Life is full of adventures. Most things are fun, but some things can make you scared. It's hard to feel brave if you don't like the dark, or going to new places. It can be easier to stay at home than to try new things or make new friends.

Grown-ups sometimes forget what it's like to feel frightened. Show them this book and talk about what makes you scared. Then they will know how to help you feel better.

Everybody gets a bit scared sometimes. You can learn how to get rid of that feeling, and then you can carry on having fun adventures!

Lots of people are afraid of the dark. They hear strange noises and see shapes in the shadows.

Don't let your imagination make you scared. Think about your favourite things until you fall asleep.

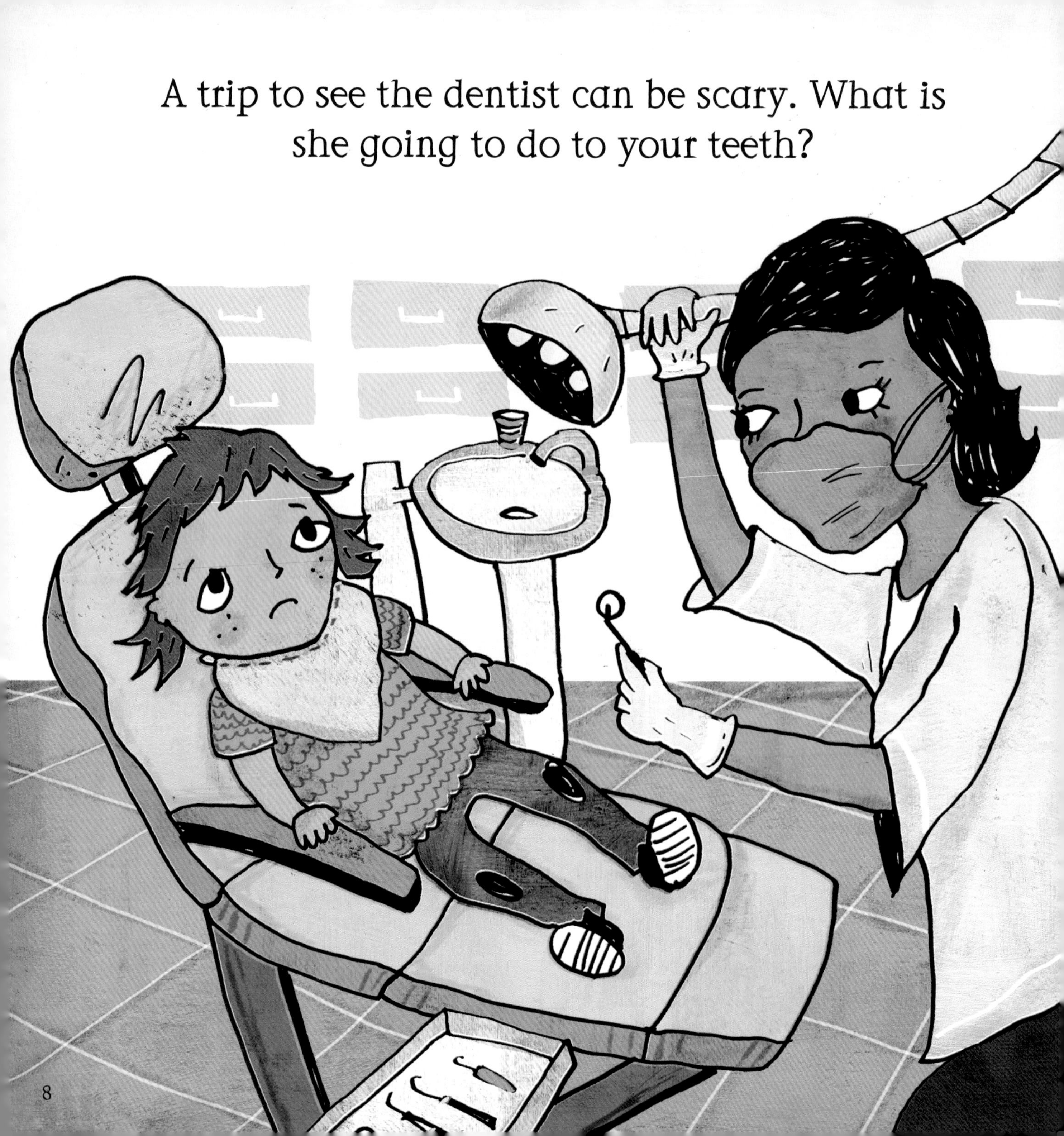

A trip to see the dentist can be scary. What is she going to do to your teeth?

The dentist sees people like you every day. She will be very gentle. It only takes two minutes to check that your teeth are healthy.

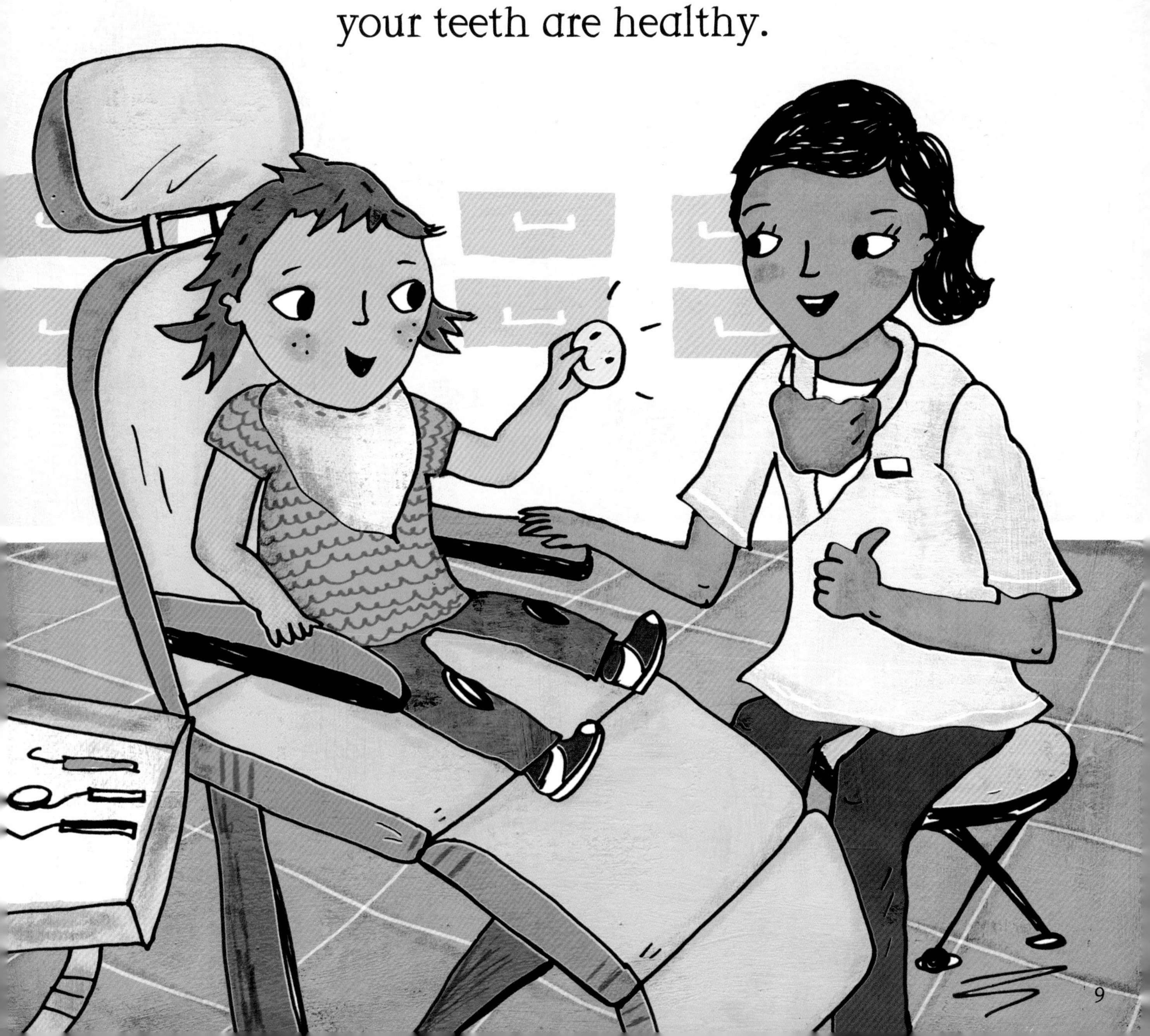

Your first day at school might make you scared. The people and the place are all new. How will you know what to do?

Everyone is scared when they do something for the first time. Listen carefully and your teacher will tell you all you need to know.

Your friend is having a swimming party. You don't want to go because you're afraid of the water.

Find a friend who wants to stay at the shallow end. You can play safely together and you won't miss the party fun!

You have been invited to your friend's house for a sleepover. But you've never spent the night away from home!

Tell your friend's parents that you are scared. They will do everything they can to make you feel happy and safe.

You're in the school play and everyone is looking at you. What if you do something wrong, or fall over and look silly?

Think about what you are doing, and you shouldn't go wrong. If you do, just smile and carry on. No one thinks you are silly.

Lucky you! You have a new pet rabbit to play with. But you're scared he's going to get ill one day.

Don't worry about something that hasn't happened yet. Your rabbit will have a very happy life if you feed him and care for him.

You want to join in the games in the playground, but you're scared that nobody likes you. What if they leave you out?

It's much easier to make friends if you try to join in. Find the person you know best and stay next to them at first.

Notes for Parents and Caregivers

This series of books has been written to help you to help your child understand that strong feelings are a natural part of life, and that, with help from you, they can learn to manage their own feelings and responses to others.

Feeling Scared is a book to share with your child. It is suitable for children from four years old, but you will still find it useful when your child is much older.

Strong feelings are a natural part of being human, and of developing relationships with others. Your child needs your help as he or she learns to manage their feelings without losing control or self-esteem. When your child feels cross, sad, shy, frustrated, angry, jealous or scared, you will understandably be concerned. But you don't have to wait until there is a crisis in your child's life or relationships before starting to help by reading this book - your child will be able to concentrate much better when they are calm.

Here are some general tips about using this book:

- Don't rush to read this book when your child is distressed. At this time they probably need a hug, a quiet time with you, or a favourite soft toy.
- For the first time, always read the book together, so your child understands what it is about. Then you can leave it for them to come back to in their own time.
- Choose a comfortable place, where you can sit together without being interrupted.
- Avoid distractions (TV, radio etc).
- Choose a calm and quiet time. Bedtime is ideal, as your child will be feeling relaxed, warm and comfy.
- If you have more than one child, read the book as a family. It's best not to single out one child. We all need help with managing our feelings, and brothers and sisters sometimes offer really helpful advice and comments.
- If your child seems bored or troubled by the book, stop and do something else. You could read a different book or talk about what you have been doing during the day.

Using this book

Here are some notes you could follow when reading this book with your child.

Read the title of the book, and look at the cover picture. Tell your child that the book is about feeling scared, and the children in the book need their help to stop feeling frightened. Even if your child hasn't ever felt scared, it may help them to understand their friends or other children they meet, who may be easily scared.

Tell your child that everyone feels scared sometimes, and this may make you feel lonely or sad, or cry and want your mum, and all these responses are quite normal, even for grown-ups. Your child needs to know that there is nothing wrong with feeling a bit scared, but it helps to talk about what they could do when they feel scared again.

The first two pages of the book will help you to talk about feeling frightened, and some of the physical and emotional effects of this. Perhaps you could tell your child about a time when you felt scared (on a roller coaster, doing your driving test, having an operation), talk about how you felt and what you did.

The rest of the book describes some situations that can make children feel frightened or anxious. As you look at each left hand page, before you read the words, see if your child can spot what is making the child in the book feel scared, and what is happening in the picture. Say 'Who do you think is feeling scared in this picture? Why do you think they are scared?"

Before you read the right hand page, ask your child how they could help the frightened child by suggesting something they could do. Try to be positive about every suggestion, they may find it difficult at first, and older siblings might be able to help with ideas.

When you have finished reading the book, give your child a hug, tell them they are a good problem solver, and leave the book where they can return to it later.

Sally Featherstone